Finding the Way

D0415363

FINDING THE WAY

A Tao
For Down-to-Earth People

Susan Montag

Photographs by Phillip Augusta

Foreword by Lon Milo DuQuette

Nicolas-Hays, Inc.
Berwick, Maine

WANDSWORTH LIBRARY SERVICE

First published in 2005 by
Nicolas-Hays, Inc.
P. O. Box 1126
Berwick, ME 03901-1126
www.nicolashays.com

Distributed to the trade by
Red Wheel/Weiser, LLC
P. O. Box 612
York Beach, ME 03910-0612
www.redwheelweiser.com

Text copyright © 2005 by Susan Montag. Interior photographs copyright © Phillip Augusta. All rights reserved. No part of this publication may be reproduced or transmitted in any form or by any means, electronic or mechanical, including photocopying, recording, or by any information storage and retrieval system, without permission in writing from Nicolas-Hays, Inc. Reviewers may quote brief passages.

Library of Congress Cataloging-in-Publication Data available on request.

Cover and text design by Phillip Augusta.
Typeset in Caxton
VG
Printed in the United States of America
11   10   09   08   07   06   05
7   6   5   4   3   2   1

The paper used in this publication meets the minimum requirements of the American National Standard for Information Sciences—Permanence of Paper for Printed Library Materials Z39.48–1992 (R1997).

LONDON BOROUGH OF WANDSWORTH	
501398314	
Askews	15-May-2008
299.51482 MONT	£9.99
	WWX0003134/0012

Dedicated to the memory of Russell Castillo, 1946–1978

I would like to thank my husband Roger Ziemann for his encouragement and support, and my teachers Larry Sutin and Scott Edelstein for their guidance on this project.

Foreword

by Lon Milo DuQuette

It is probably a serious breach of scholarly decorum to begin a Foreword to another author's work by writing about oneself. In this case, I hope to be forgiven for my lapse into spiritual narcissism for, in truth, I have been touched and deeply identify with what I perceive to be the spirit of this marvelous work—a work that (if names and labels did not serve only to confuse matters) could be described as "*Western* Eastern thought."

I'm a westerner. I say this not as a boast or an apology. It's just a fact. I was born in California and raised in the Midwest. My parents were of western European and Native American stock. I was noisily raised in an archetypically dysfunctional family of good Methodists in the archetypically dysfunctional universe of 1950s–60s small-town Nebraska (advertised as the place "Where the West Begins!"). Back then, there were no minority groups in town—no Jews, no Buddhists, no Hindus, or Muslims. Nobody spoke about "Eastern thought" or "Western thought." As a matter of fact, in small-town Nebraska nobody spoke about "thought" at all; and, until I moved back (west) to California to go to college, I believed that the act of *not thinking about thought* was the "Western way."

The psychedelic revolution of the mid-1960s radically changed my thinking on this subject and most everything else. Almost overnight, I realized with Technicolor® certainty that human consciousness— my consciousness—was an awesome and holy thing, perhaps the most important thing in the universe. I wasn't in Nebraska anymore—and my newly-awakened third eye turned toward the east in search of more light.

I found it almost immediately in the form of a tiny book that I bought at my college bookstore for 95 cents. It bore the curious two-part title, *Lao Tzu—Tao Te Ching*,[1] and advertised itself as ". . . the principal classic in the thought of Taoism."[2]

The translator's very lengthy and scholarly Introduction was of no interest to me. My craving for instant spiritual gratification was too strong. I thumbed straight to the opening lines of the text itself and sipped my first ambrosial taste of "Eastern thought."

> The way that can be told
> Is not the constant way;
> The name that can be named
> Is not the constant name.
>
> The nameless was the beginning
> of heaven and earth;
> The named was the mother of the
> myriad creatures.[3]

What beauty! It was perfect—so perfectly simple; 40 words describing what cannot be described—the infinitely simple, nameless *Way Things Are.* Forget about deities, saviors, and devils, or sin, guilt, reward, and punishment. Those are things with names, and names separate everything from the pure, nameless *Way Things Are.*

For a moment I stopped breathing. It was as if I had ingested a spiritual drug and was pausing to see if I would explode, or turn purple, or die, or giggle.

Of course I didn't do any of those things (well, maybe I giggled a little). After a few months of reading and re-reading the text and meditating upon its inscrutable words, I resolved to discard completely the faith of my fathers and try my hand at becoming a first-rate Eastern mystic. For a few years, I didn't do such a bad job. I left the world of psychedelics, started seriously practicing yoga and the obligatory meditative practices, and began a systematic study of the *I Ching*.

Yes sir, I had great spiritual goals. I was going to be egoless. I was going to be the most egoless mystic in town. I envisioned my egoless self quietly gaining illumination while poised egolessly by the coy pond, my legs locked in a flawless lotus position, my eyes firmly fixed upon the center of my egoless forehead, my shaved head gleaming in the leaf-filtered sunlight of my cool and tranquil Zen garden.

Man! I was going to look *so cool* without an ego!

Obviously something wasn't right, and it was more than just my battle with the ego. It was a battle with how I was hardwired. It was as though I was trying to run Eastern software on my Western hardware. It was then I began to examine the nature of my Western psyche and the differences between the Eastern and Western approaches to enlightenment.

No matter what some of the pundits of each school may preach, the goals are the same; supreme illumination and absorption into godhead. But the ways the Eastern and Western mystic go about achieving that goal are as different as yin and yang, in and out.

The spiritual sciences of the East encourage the individual to simplify—to turn *inward* to discover the true nature of self and deity. By stilling the body and mind, and systematically striping away the illusionary veils of sensations, desires, and ego, the Eastern mystic eventually reaches the moment when something snaps—the mind is transcended, and he or she is absorbed into what is poorly described as wall-to-wall *emptiness.*

Conversely, by nature Western mystics are inclined to seek *externally* for the answers. Consider how we in the West are so obedient to scripture and complex doctrines—so attracted to ritual, priestly crafts, and prayerful appeals to a God apparently outside of ourselves and nature. Under the right circumstances, however, these outward things can trigger in the devotee an illumination that "fills the soul" with the presence of deity—something snaps—the mind is transcended, and the consciousness of the Western mystic is absorbed into what can be poorly described as wall-to-wall *fullness.*

Realizing that the two supreme goals are one and the same—that subjective reality lives in objective things and actions—left me in a most awkward and frustrating position: the lonesome, inside-out bipolarity of the *Western* Eastern mystic. Fortunately, I would eventually bring this malady under control by heavily self-medicating with the concepts and practices of the "Zen of the West"—the Hermetic Qabalah,[4] tarot, and ceremonial magick.

These highly esoteric Western traditions are not for everyone. Indeed, for centuries they have been branded as heretical by the Western spiritual "authorities" who have (for reasons both understandable and despicable) either found themselves unable to appreciate the subtleties of the practices, or else have been frustrated in their attempts to successfully exploit the practices for profit or crowd control. If not for my background in Eastern thought, I, too, would have dismissed the mystic arts of the West as dangerous and superstitious nonsense.

All this being said, it remains a mystery why, as a meat-and-potatoes Midwestern Methodist teenager, I was immediately and profoundly zapped by the *Tao Te Ching*, or why, for the most part, my zeal to share its wisdom with others of my occidental ilk met with no success at all.

"Don't you get it?" became my mantra of frustration.

"No. I don't. It's just fortune-cookie double talk. How can I believe in that?"

"It's not something you *believe* in, it's the *way things are!*"

"What's so holy about things the way they are?

"No. Not about things the *way they are* . . . it's about the *way*. Don't you get it? Focusing on the *things* is how everything got all screwed up."

"I don't get it. How's that going to get me into heaven!?"

(Insert sound of my hand slapping my own forehead here.)

Obviously, it's almost impossible to be an enthusiastic proselytizer of the Tao without departing embarrassingly far from the Way the moment you open your mouth. Handing a curious friend or a relative a translation (even a very good translation) is at best a hit-or-miss affair. For thirty-five years, I've bemoaned the fact that someone, some *Western* Eastern mystic with a masterful grasp of the spirit of the text and the ability to render it into straightforward, down-to-earth English, has not done the job.

I lament no longer. I have found the English language jewel I've been seeking my entire adult life—a jewel I can share with everyone I know who insists they *don't get it.* Exactly how she did it, I cannot say. However, one thing is abundantly clear to me. By writing *Finding the Way*, Susan Montag has demonstrated in the clearest, most comfortable manner imaginable that she has truly found the Way.

Notes

1. D.C. Lau, trans. *Lau Tzu—Tao Te Ching* (Baltimore, MD: Penguin Books, 1963, latest reprint, 1985).
2. *Ibid.*, back cover material.
3. *Ibid.*, p. 57.
4. Spelled *Qabalah* to differentiate it from its overtly parochial cousins, the Hebrew Kabbalah or the Christian Cabala.

Introduction

When I tell people that I wrote my own interpretation of the *Tao Te Ching*, I'm often asked, "What is that?" There are two answers I can give: the short, easy answer, or the long, complicated one. Of course, I always give the short, easy answer, which goes something like this: The *Tao Te Ching* is the second most translated book in the world, second only to the Bible. It was written around 500 B.C.E., or about 2,500 years ago, in China, and the author is said to be someone named Lao Tzu. No one knows for sure who Lao Tzu was; it is likely that he was more than one person.[1] The word *tao* (pronounced "dow") is one of the most basic words in the Chinese language. It can mean many things, including path, way, method, system, or structure. It can also mean the reality of all things. The *Tao Te Ching* then, is a collection of sayings, poems, and proverbs, divided into 81 verses, dealing with the nature of life.

Naturally, people also want to know what lead me to do this work. Why did I, a woman who has lived most of her life in the rural Midwest, decide to spend my time in this way, creating my own take on an ancient Chinese book? The answer to that, I think, is an interesting story.

My relationship with the *Tao Te Ching* is personal rather than academic. I am not a Chinese scholar. I call myself, first and foremost, a writer. Yes, I have had a lifelong interest in matters of philosophy and religion, but I was inspired to start this project after

I found the books left behind by my late uncle, Russell Castillo.

Russ, who was my father's twin brother, died when his small sailboat capsized in the Gulf of Mexico in January of 1978. He was an expert sailing enthusiast, but the storm that came up was unexpected, and it caught him off guard after he set sail from Naples to Sanibel Island. I was ten years old when Russ died. I know enough about human nature to know that we tend to idolize our dead, but I stand by my memories of my uncle as an exceptional person. He worked as a brakeman for Burlington-Northern Railroad, and, as are many working-class men in his age range, he was a Vietnam veteran. He was a tall man. I once saw him bump his head on a door frame as he tried to pass through. But despite this intimidating exterior, he was known for his gentle ways, for his intellectual curiosity, and his patience. I believe people when they say, "I never heard Russ say a bad thing about anyone."

To know what a person read during his life is to know an intimate detail about him; it is to know what he had on his mind. This is why, when I discovered the books that belonged to Russ, twenty-five years after his death, I felt a sense of privilege. This collection of books, more than anything, was a testament to who he was. Many of the books were about the ocean or sailing. He had novels and short story collections and *Foxfire* books. He also had two translations of the *Tao Te Ching*.

The harder someone tries to figure out what the *Tao Te Ching* is about, the more confused she is likely to become. That confusion is part of the long complicated answer that I rarely attempt to give. There is no agreement among scholars about what Taoism really is, so far be it from me to try to pin it down. I will make a bold suggestion, though, and say that, to me, Taoism is a state of mind. It is about living in such a way that your problems are solved before they become problems. It is about responding to others with compassion, and about living simply. In remembering my uncle, and in hearing people relate their memories of him, it seems that he had achieved this state of mind.

When I found those two translations of the *Tao Te Ching* among my uncle's books, I knew that he had been drawn to the verses because they reflected some of his own natural gentleness. I was excited by the implications of this discovery, and wanted to share my excitement with my family. I bought copies of the *Tao Te Ching* and mailed them off to my brother, sister, and my parents.

My enthusiasm was dampened, though, by their responses, or perhaps, by their lack of response. The phrase, "Say what?" sums it up pretty well. The *Tao Te Ching* is known for many things—its poetry, its mystery, its beauty—but not, I'm afraid, for its clarity of meaning. And there may be people who would argue that it should be mysterious rather than clear, because, as it is often said about the Tao, "The way that you can say is not the way." Yet, I was frustrated. Inside the mystery, inside the poetry and the beauty, there is meaning. I could not help but believe that this stuff was meant to be used, not just pondered, and for it to be used, people had to know what it said.

It was with these thoughts in mind that I started to do the work. In all honesty, I first intended my interpretation to be only a gift to my family. I considered myself not just to be in service, as a scribe, to the *Tao Te Ching*, but to be in service to my uncle as well, giving my family the opportunity to get the same message that I had gotten. It was only after I showed the work in progress to several people, and was greeted with an enthusiastic response, that it occurred to me that what I was doing might be of interest to many people, not just my relatives.

I worked from existing English translations of the *Tao Te Ching*. I used the books that had belonged to my uncle (the Witter Bynner and the Gia-Fu Feng translations), as well as many others that I accumulated as the project progressed. I compared the verses of one translation to another, developing a method somewhat like the Miller Analogy Test, which requires the test taker to look for relationships between words.

It was the relationship that determined what words I myself chose to use. My goal was, first and foremost, clarity; but at times I found the verses falling into rhythms and sometimes rhymes. When that felt natural, I let it happen. Those familiar with the *Tao Te Ching* will see that some of the well-known metaphors are missing. My intent was to maintain the spirit of those metaphors but to replace them with others that are useful in the context of the modern world. I also chose not to use the world "Tao" in the verses, but rather the phrase "Way of Life." Always, my intent was to make the ideas accessible to a wide range of readers.

When I think of this book, I'm amazed most by the way it came about. The events themselves seem to have something of the *Tao Te Ching* in them, both a beginning and an end, both joy and sorrow, life and death. I think my uncle would have liked this work I have done. In a big way, it is his work, too. I have him to thank for leaving those books behind for me to discover twenty-five years after his death, and for being who he was. It was his own down-to-earth way that helped me to see the gentle and compassionate message of the *Tao Te Ching*.

This is what I hope to share with those who find their way to this book.

Notes

1. Witter Bynner, *The Way of Life According to Lao Tzu, Chuang Tzu and Seng Tsan* (Fremont, CA: Jain, 2000), pp. 9–10.

One

Before we invented language,
    there were no words to say one thing
      was different from another thing.
That means that all the differences
    of the world were invented by people.
A person who is all prim and serious
    is exactly the same
      as one who goes around
        swearing and acting rowdy.
The only reason one is respected
    and the other is not
      is because words were invented
        to say one is better than the other.
Instead of saying one is good and one is bad,
    it would make more sense to say,
      "That is just the Way of Life,"
        because all things are part
          of the Way of Life,
            and the Way of Life is in all things.

Two

If you say you like one thing best,
   that must mean you like other things less.
If you say, "This is my good kid,"
   the other kid you have must be the bad one.
Life and death seem like opposites of each other.
But have you ever thought
   that you can't have one without the other?
Do you understand that without "difficult,"
   "easy" does not exist?
Without long, there is no short?
Without high, there is no low?

Think about this:
If all people could sing beautifully,
   no one would have a beautiful singing voice.
Singing would be like the air:
   we would not notice it.
Therefore, only a foolish person
   hates another person for being different.
If each person was the same as every
   other person,
      we would all disappear.

Three

Don't feel like you are a good person
just because you own a lot of things.
If owning things is what it takes
to be a good person,
people will want to take away
the things you own
so they can be good people, too.
Instead of causing envy,
let people feel complete.
Let them know what they know,
and share what you have to eat.
They will grow strong and content
so they'll need to take no action,
and when people take no action
the work of peace has been done.

Four

Once, nothing existed.
But within the nothing,
there was the potential
for all things.
That means that "Nothing"
was the mother of "Everything."
That is why we naturally think in opposites—
smooth opposed to rough,
bright opposed to dim,
windy opposed to calm.
But where did this Nothing come from?
This is a thing I cannot answer.

Five

The Way of Life has no prejudice;
it treats all people the same.
If you are wise, you will understand
what this means.
No matter how much money you have,
no matter how carefully
you have lived your life,
you still can't breathe under water;
you still won't be able to fly
if you fall off the roof.

Life is like the sail of a boat.
The Way of Life is like the wind
that blows it one way and then the other.
It would be pretty stupid to stand there and wonder
if a sail is full of wind, or if it is empty of wind
when anyone can see
it has to be empty on one side
to be full on the other.
Life, too, has to be empty in order to be full.

Six

The Way of Life never dies.
It is the energy of everything.
It is like a mother who gives birth
   to all things, over and over again,
   with each tick of the clock.

Seven

The reason the Way of Life does not die
is because It cannot be defined.
When something cannot be defined, it lasts forever.
So if a man is wise, he will not go around saying
he is one thing and not another.
He will say that he is all things,
good and bad, religious and irreligious,
smart and stupid, serious and silly.
That way he is not tied
to any one definition of himself
and he can live as if he has a direct connection
to the Way of Life.

Eight

When water fills a sink,
  it is in the shape of a sink,
  and when it fills a glass,
    it is in the shape of the glass.
If we lived our lives as naturally as water flows,
  we would find the right shape with no effort.
We would live with clear hearts,
  and we would get along with our neighbors.
We would find no reason to tell lies,
  and we would take good care of the earth.
Our governments would run
  like they were invisible,
    and companies would never try to cheat people.
Everyone would find the work
  they were born to do,
    and no one would feel the need
      to stand in any other person's way
      or to point accusing fingers
        at their sisters and brothers.

Nine

Would it make sense to sharpen a knife
until the blade disappeared?
Everyone knows the answer is no,
but other excesses are just as foolish.

Think of how good a piece of chocolate tastes
if you have one now and then.
But if you eat a pound of chocolate every day,
it becomes as tasteless as paper.
Gluttony is an idiot that kills the thing it loves.

Ten

If you can live without saying
one thing is different from another thing,
then you will be as open-minded
as a newborn baby.
You will be able to love anybody
without noticing a thing about them.
You will be able to let the Way of Life
take root inside you as if you were its mother
instead of the other way around.
You will be able to think
with the wholeness
of your mind and body and soul
instead of with just the facts
of your education.
You will do good work
because you love to do good work—
not because you want a paycheck—
and you will guide people wisely
without their noticing
what you have done.

Eleven

When you buy a vase,
 you are paying for the pretty glass
  but also for the empty space inside.
If that space were filled with glass,
 you could not put a flower into it.

The empty space of a door
 is the useful part of the door,
  and the empty space of the window
   is the valuable part of the window.
People are able to use what is there
 only because of what is not there.

Twelve

You do not see the world
in the same way a hawk sees it.
The way you smell the world
is not the way a cat smells it.
You don't hear the world
in the way a dog hears the world.
In fact, no one person
sees or hears or smells
the world in exactly the way
any other person does.

Two people can argue forever
about the way the world is or is not,
but those people will never get any closer
to the truth.
There is no right way to perceive.
The wise woman understands
that she has her own world,
and she lets other people have theirs.

Thirteen

If your happiness is attached to success,
success becomes a burden
that has to be maintained,
so it kills your happiness.
That is why rich and famous people
aren't always happy.

So don't think in terms of success and failure.
Instead, just do your work.
Don't make an emotional issue out of it.
Say to yourself,
"Whether I succeed or fail,
it is all the same to me."
When people see that you are concerned
with doing good work
and not with big ideas of success
they will see that you are
offering them wisdom.

Fourteen

The beginning of time and the end of time
are both invisible and silent.
The beginning and end of time
cannot be pinpointed,
because they do not exist.
Since neither exists, both are zeros,
and one zero is the same as any other zero.
So the beginning and end of time
are the same thing.
If you try to find the beginning,
or if you fret about the end,
your efforts and worries will bring zero.
But if you understand that the beginning
and the end are the same
thing,
you will see that each moment of time
contains both of them.
You will see that just by being
alive in this moment,
you have lived forever.

Fifteen

Long ago there were people
who lived by a profound wisdom.
Because they were so wise,
they are hard to describe.

They lived as carefully as travelers
crossing a frozen river,
as quietly as considerate neighbors at night.
They lived as politely as formal visitors,
and they were as quick to give in
as the melting of thin ice.
They lived as simply as uncarved wood,
they were as open as a cave—
yet they were as mysterious as murky water
in the way that they behaved.

How could they be all these things?
By not demanding satisfaction.
By not demanding it,
they found it everywhere.

Sixteen

Try to live as peacefully as a blade of grass.
A blade of grass sprouts and lives,
    then it returns to earth,
        giving way to other blades of grass.
It never worries about itself.
Some people might think it is better
    to rage against life and death,
        but raging against life and death
          denies the reality of all existence.
Denial is like living with a blindfold on.
Acceptance will allow you to live with open eyes.
If your eyes are open, your mind will be open.
If your mind is open, your heart will be open.
If your heart is open, you will be
    a leader among people.
A true leader behaves as naturally as
    the Way of Life.
The Way of Life contains
    both the beginning and the end,
        so if you behave as naturally as the Way,
      you will find that your life
        is never-ending.

Seventeen

The best leaders are not politicians,
because they are never elected.
The best leaders lead from where
they live and work,
so quietly they are barely noticed.
Politicians rise to power because
they smile and shake hands
and do a lot of double-talk.
Even if people love them,
they are not the best leaders we have.
The worse leaders of all, elected or not,
come to power by using fear tactics,
with the goal of imposing
their will on others.

If your leaders do not trust you
to make your own decisions,
you should not trust your leaders.

But if your leaders guide you to success
with just a word or two,
and then say that you
have succeeded on your own,
you should keep those leaders
because they understand
the Way of Life.

Eighteen

A long time ago, people did not need laws,
  because they knew the Way of Life
  without even thinking about it.

If we could get back to that point,
  we wouldn't need to talk about kindness
  or morality,
    because all people would be
    kind and moral already.

If we got back to the Way of Life,
  we would not need to talk about wisdom,
  because all people would be wise.

The words *kind* and *moral*
  would have no meaning,
    and they would disappear.

Because we have forgotten the Way of Life,
  we need these words.
We need governments and religions
  to turn the words into laws,
    and we need ministers and police
    to check up on people.

No one likes to get into trouble,
  so when people can't follow the rules,
    they pretend they can follow
    instead of telling the truth.

When pretending replaces the Way of Life,
  hypocrites are honored,
    and honest people are seen as immoral.

— 23 —

Nineteen

If a man tells you he went to the best college,
  that does not mean he knows a thing
    about the Way of Life.
He would be smarter to stop pretending
  that education
    is about getting a piece of paper.
If a man tells you he acts with duty and honor,
  that does not mean he knows a thing
    about the Way of Life.
His family would be more fortunate if
  he took care of them
    just because he loved them.
If a man tells you he makes a lot of money,
  that does not mean he knows a thing
    about the Way of Life.
He would be better off to find
  no meaning in wealth;
    then he would not have to worry about
    having it stolen from him.

Why concern yourself with education,
  duty, and money?
The Way of Life can set you free
  to learn in earnest,
    to embrace your true nature,
      to find joy in what you have.

Twenty

Everyone talks about the importance
of a good education,
but what does that really mean?
If all you are doing is memorizing facts,
you are learning nothing.
Books on a shelf are full of facts
that anyone can look up any time.
If all you are doing is letting others tell you
what to think,
you are still learning nothing.
Accepting a teacher's definitions of good and bad,
his notions of true and false,
letting him tell you which ideas to fear and
which to embrace,
is not education at all.
When people are well educated,
they get to live lives of easy consumption,
while I, because of lack of education,
am a vagrant, as powerless as a child.
When people become wise and moral,
they deserve to pile up belongings,
while I, a stupid low-life, have nothing.
What an idiot I must be to not join in
this memorization of facts!
What a loser!
While these important people of the world
buy expensive cars and build huge houses,
I drift along going nowhere,
a head full of nothing,
with only the world as my dinner,
and only the stars of heaven
as my drink.

— 25 —

Twenty-One

The way to be a virtuous person
  is to simply follow the Way of Life.
The Way of Life cannot be seen or touched,
  yet within It is all that appears before you.
The Way of Life cannot be touched or seen,
  yet within It is all you can reach.
The Way of Life is a jar full of darkness,
  yet within is the light that makes flowers grow,
    the desire of a lover's touch,
      and the sound of children singing.
Flowers and lovers and children are very real—
  to believe in them requires an effortless faith.
From the beginning of time until now
  the Way of Life has not faltered
    in the work of creating them.
The evidence is all around us.

What more do I need to believe
  in the Way of Life than this?

Twenty-Two

Surrender and you will have won the game,
give in to others and you will get your way.
Desire nothing you can't have,
and you will find that you have
all that you want.
If you are happy with the money in your pocket,
you are richer than people with great wealth
who are miserable because they always
want more.
Understanding this, a wise woman embraces
simple things
and her life becomes a good example
for everyone.
She does not show off with big diamonds,
but shines like a diamond herself.
She does not command people to do as she says,
but through her actions shows them
what to do.
She does not value herself over other people,
and therefore people sing her praises.
So when I say "surrender and you will have
won the game,"
that is not just double-talk.
It means only that you should be
honest and kind,
and good things will come to you naturally.

Twenty-Three

Weather does not ask for permission—
it just does what it needs to do.
If it needs to rain, it rains,
if it needs to snow, it snows.
If the weather does not have to ask
for permission to exist,
why should you worry
about your right to exist?
If you are a follower of the Way of Life,
you will understand that your presence
is no less righteous than the rain.
If you lose the Way of Life,
you will feel anxiety when people glace at you,
and you will imagine
they want you to go away.
But if you find the Way of Life again,
you will see only a glance in a glance.
You will smile and say hello,
and people will believe you belong there.
But if you continue to imagine
that no one likes you
and you pout about it and act like a jerk,
people will treat you like you are a jerk.
Behave toward others the way you want them
to behave toward you.

Twenty-Four

If you walk around like you
  are something special,
    someone will try to prove that you are not.
If you walk around like you
  are in a big important hurry,
    someone will make sure to get in your way.
If you constantly point out your own goodness,
  people will try to catch you
    doing something unethical.
If you go on and on all the time about
  your accomplishments,
    people will disappear
      when they see you coming
        because they will find you
          to be an incredible bore.
According to the Way of Life,
  none of these things brings happiness;
    they just make people not like you.
Therefore, a wise person avoids
  these kinds of behaviors.

Twenty-Five

Something mysteriously formed
before anything else could form.
Nothing has ever been added to it
or taken away.
It has never changed—
all things that have ever existed
have come from this mystery.
Since it was the only thing there,
it had to be both the mother and father
of all things.
Though any words that I call
this mother and father
are words that I have made up,
I've called it here "the Way of Life."
Maybe I should have called it "Infinity."
I could call it infinity
because infinity flows and flows
out into the universe, on and on,
going so far away that it comes
back to us,
and the beginning becomes the end.
That means the Way of Life is infinite,
the universe is infinite,
and the earth is infinite.
People who live naturally are also infinite.
These four things are like a circle of power:
People who live naturally follow the earth;
the earth follows the universe;
the universe follows the Way of Life;
and the Way of Life
follows what is natural.

Twenty-Six

Order is the master of chaos;
   organization is the keeper of creativity;
    calmness is the container of joy.
So as you go about your business,
   pay attention to what you are doing
    and act like a mature
    and reasonable person.
You don't need to get overly excited
   if something good happens.
If you follow the Way of Life,
   you'll feel no need to jump up and down
    about one little thing,
      because all good things
      were already yours.

Twenty-Seven

If someone does her work well enough,
   she never has to redo it.
She never has to retrace her footsteps
   to find out where things went wrong,
      or to apologize for making careless remarks.
A person who follows the Way of Life
   sees her work in all things.
Therefore, if she wants to do the work perfectly,
   she doesn't abandon people on the wayside.
She feels a responsibility to teach people who
   need to learn.
But if she is insightful enough,
   when she sees someone misbehaving
      she will look for
         the cause of the misbehavior
            in her own correct behavior.
She will remember that misbehaving people
   are teachers of well-behaved people,
      as much as the other way around.
If she insists that she is the only teacher,
   she is not a real follower of the Way of Life.

You would be better off to follow the example
   of the misbehaving one.

Twenty-Eight

If you are a man, don't be afraid to be gentle,
and if you are woman, don't be afraid
to be strong.
It is best for all people to have both traits.
Since the Way of Life needed both
gentleness and strength
to create you within Itself,
you need both gentleness and strength
to create the Way of Life
within yourself.
If you allow opposite traits to exist inside you,
you will be the mirror image of the
Way of Life.

You should try to be the best person you can be,
but also the most humble.
Think about yourself as a valley,
A valley has a low point,
but only because it is surrounded
by higher ground.
You should have both high ground
and low ground,
because otherwise you are flat,
and if you are flat there is no place
for the river to flow.

Twenty-Nine

Why fight over who owns the whole world?
By fighting over it, you'll just ruin it.
And what is the point
   of owning the whole world?
Can you put up a fence that big?
If you owned the moon,
   could you prevent others from looking at it?
History shows that people who have power
   eventually are made to obey,
         that people who are allowed to speak
         are eventually made to shut up,
            and that people with wealth
               eventually become poor.
All vice-versa as well.
The opposite of moderation is just moderation.
That's why it is best to live that way.

Thirty

If you get the chance to talk
  to the leader of your country,
What should you say?
You should tell him not to use weapons
  to take over the world.
Tell him that whatever weapons he invents
  will find their way
    into the hands of the enemy.
Tell him that the spoils of war are hardship.
A good leader finds more triumph
  in preventing battles than in winning them.
A good leader is never motivated
  by selfishness and glory.
He does only what must be done,
  taking no delight in military victory.
This kind of victory is not the Way of Life.
If you love to kill, you're dead.

Thirty-One

The best weapons demonstrate the best of hate.
A follower of the Way of Life
    never willingly takes up arms
        because he places peace above all rewards.
If he is forced to defend himself against war
    he sees no bravery or triumph in his acts,
        knowing that a willingness to kill
            shows the death of one's self.
It is a sign of terrible times
    when good people pick up weapons.
Good people conduct war as if
    conducting their own funerals
        and they celebrate war victories
            with only tears.

Thirty-Two

The Way of Life goes on forever
and is forever undefined.
Even though It is as simple as uncut wood,
you cannot control It.
But if someone could control the Way of Life,
all things would obey her.
She could tell the fields to grow
and they would grow.
She would say "peace,"
and there would be peace.
Schools would close,
because she would say "Learn,"
and all people would know
what they needed to know.
People would quickly see each other as equals,
so distinctions between them would disappear.
That is the way it was
before we named everything.
Once we started to name things,
we didn't know where to stop.
Once we named differences,
we had to learn to be tolerant, and to forgive.
Tolerance welcomes people no matter
what category they fit.
The Way of Life
does not create categories to begin with.
Forgiveness makes note of "immorality,"
then forgets.
The Way of Life doesn't know
that immorality exists.
The Way of Life just lets people "be."
It sees them like many rivers
running into one sea.

Thirty-Three

A smart man understands
why other people do things.
The smartest man understands
why he does what he does.
Taking change of other people
is like renting a shovel,
but if you take charge of yourself,
the shovel is your own.
If you are in charge of yourself,
you won't go into debt
buying things you don't need.
You won't wander around trying to
"find yourself,"
because you'll always know
right where you are.

Thirty-Four

We all depend on the Way of Life,
  and It never lets us down.
It never calls in sick, which is a good thing,
  because if the Way of Life called in sick,
    we would all disappear—
      even the most important people
      in the town.
But how could the Way of Life call in sick?
It never leaves Its post.
It keeps working, morning, noon, and night,
  never complaining, never asking to be paid.
It makes our blood pump,
  It gives us air for our lungs,
    It makes the food for our stomachs—
      yet most of the time we, ignore It.
Think how much we would thank a host
  who not only could make birds sing for us,
    but is the one that made our ears work
    to hear them!
How silly of us to brag of our deeds,
  when the Way of Life silently does these.

Thirty-Five

If you are a follower of the Way of Life,
you'll befriend everyone you meet—
they'll be drawn to ring your doorbell
as if invited to a feast.
But don't worry what you'll feed them—
just fill them up with peace.

Thirty-Six

If you feel insulted by a remark,
　you must have first shown your pride.
If you are embarrassed by failure,
　you must have first told everyone
　　of your success.
If you feel that you have been stripped
　of what is rightfully yours,
　　you must have first displayed your wealth.
It is natural for power and money
　to change hands,
　　so if you go around showing off all you have,
　　　people will know right where to get it.
That is why a wise man never flaunts
　his success and privilege;
　　to do so is to be like a shiny fish,
　　　teasing the fisherman.

Thirty-Seven

The Way of Life doesn't schedule things
   on a calendar.
It doesn't rush around to meet Its goals.
But have you noticed how the Way of Life
   always gets the job done?
If our leaders operated this way,
   our governments would run as naturally
     as water runs downhill.
Laws and rules would evaporate into the air,
   and there would be peace and harmony.

Thirty-Eight

People who do good work
don't have to draw attention to it
because the work speaks for itself.
People who don't care about the work
make a big deal about how much
trouble the work is,
and in doing so, they keep themselves
from getting much of it done.

If a man sees kindness as his most important job,
he will get his work done by being good.
But if he says, "My job is to make rules
so that other people are as good as me,"
he will find that he works long
and accomplishes little.
If he says, "My job is to enforce all the rules,"
he will then mindlessly punish people
who are just living as they see fit.

When we named one thing good
and another thing bad,
we concerned ourselves with being good.

When we found out how difficult it is to be good,
we extended guidance to each other
in kindness.

When we found out how difficult it is
to be kind to others,
we made rules to remind each other
how to behave.

Once we started behaving according to rules,

we forgot why we made the
rules in the first place.

When we forgot why we made the rules,
they became rituals.

When rituals come to rule our lives,
they become more important than people,
and that is against the Way of Life.

Leaders who demand that their followers
live according to rituals
are not real leaders.
Followers of the Way of Life
stay with what is true.
They live by what makes good sense,
not by empty rules.

Thirty-Nine

Since the beginning of time,
  things have added up the same way.
All things = One thing.
This just means that all the parts
  come together to make the whole.

The clearness of the sky,
  plus the firmness of the earth,
    plus the strength of our spirits,
      add up to make our world.

So our communities need
  leaders and followers both.
A roof without a house is nothing of use,
  and leaves never grow unless there are roots.
Without people, a leader has nothing to do.

If you are leader, your job is not to control.
You are a servant—one part of a whole.

Forty

The quiet before life
   is the same quiet that comes after.
The peace before birth
   becomes our peace again.
All things of this world
   came from the thing called "existence,"
   and existence came from
     the same quiet we did.

Forty-One

Wise people, when they hear about
the Way of Life,
take that path and stay on it.
Average people get on the path,
but they don't stay.
Foolish people, hearing about the Way of Life,
laugh out loud—and laugh some more.
But if they didn't laugh,
the Way of Life would not be the Way of Life.
All people—wise, average, and foolish—
must exist to make It what It is.

To those who laugh, the Way of Life
seems like a backward path,
both hard to navigate and climb.
Top seems like bottom,
the easy way seems hard,
wealth seems like poverty,
virtue like sin:
The path that holds the most rewards
seems to hold the least of them.
But the Way of Life is a perfect circle,
and It holds eternity within.
Shapeless nothing becomes image,
senseless noise becomes the melody of song,
and in this way that makes fools laugh,
wise people walk along.

Forty-Two

The Way of Life started undivided.
It was just one big thing.
Then one became two,
  two became three,
    and so on and so on,
      until there was everything.
This "everything" goes back as well as forth.
It contains the living and the dead.
It is action and It is opposite action.
It always holds the whole,
  never just this part, or that part instead.

People who accomplish little
  don't like to say, "I'm worthless, I am low."
Yet great people often say,
  "I'm just a servant of the whole."
Many great teachers of the past
  have said exactly this:
Those who try to rule by force
  will by force be met with death.

This also will be my teaching.

Forty-Three

Water can travel through the rockiest soil;
locked doors don't keep out smoke.
Things that behave without effort
are most likely to reach their mark.

But smoke teaches in silence.
Water never teaches with rules.
That means the lessons are so easy that
the students are very few.

Forty-Four

Do you value your reputation over yourself?
Are your possessions more important
   to you than your life?
Why fret over gains and losses
   when both are equal pains.
A woman who over-spends will suffer.
One who hoards her money and wants even more
   is suffering the same.
But a woman who is content
   with either lots or little,
      feels no failure either way.
If she loses what she has,
   she simply starts again.

Forty-Five

If you are a true follower of the Way of Life,
  you will never retire from your job
    because you see your job
      as everything you say and do.
In this way, your work will
  always be complete
    and you will leave a trail of
      accomplishments wherever you go.
However, to some it will seem
  that you have done nothing at all.

When you speak with honesty,
  you'll be called a liar.
When you act with intelligence,
  you'll be called a fool.
When you are graceful,
  people will say you are awkward.
Yet, eventually your way will rule.

As naturally as people move to get warm,
  as naturally as they stay still to keep cool,
    they will come into the Way of Life.

Forty-Six

When a gardener uses a horse
to haul manure to the garden,
that is the Way of Life.
But if the gardener uses the horse
to take over her neighbors' gardens,
that is not the Way of Life.
That is selfishness and want,
greed and discontent.
Accept that enough is enough,
and you will have enough.

Forty-Seven

Don't travel the globe looking
for a window to forever.
The only forever you have
is at the center of yourself.
The further out you look,
the more lost you will become.

If you live according to the Way of Life,
you can travel without moving,
see without looking,
and do all you need to do
just by being you.

Forty-Eight

A wise guy tries to sound educated.
He speaks with certainty about everything
    and refuses to lose an argument.
A wise person listens.
He speaks with certainty about nothing,
    and is willing to consider new ideas.

To be wise,
    be certain of nothing.
When you are certain of nothing,
    you will try to do nothing.
In trying to do nothing,
    all your work is done.

How can I say that
    when you try to do nothing
        all your work is done?
Because the Way of Life
    does not try, yet does all things.

Forty-Nine

A virtuous woman will be good to good people
and she'll be good to bad people.
A virtuous man will trust truthful people
and he'll trust liars, too.
To the untrained eyes
of those who do not follow the Way of Life,
this will seem foolish,
like the naive ways of a child.
But those who follow the Way know:
to be virtuous is to see the virtue in others.

Fifty

Some people live waiting for life,
others live waiting for death.
The exceptional person
does not wait for life or death,
but lives life as it happens.
He breathes in life with each breath
and eats life for every meal.

In each moment there is beginning
and there is end.
Be present in the moment
and you live forever.
Let yourself be full of life,
and you have no place for death to enter.

Fifty-One

All things come from the Way of Life.
They feed on its goodness,
   are shaped by its nature,
      are cared for, protected, comforted.

The Way of Life creates
   without concern for reward.
You, too, should concern yourself
   with the benefit of others
      rather than their obedience.
This is virtue.

Fifty-Two

The Way of Life is the mother of all things.
That means that all things
　　are sons and daughters of the Way of Life.
If you know the sons and daughters,
　　you know the mother,
　　　　and if you know the mother,
　　　　　　you know eternity.
How can you come to know
　　the sons and daughters of the Way?
Don't run your mouth all the time.
Don't believe everything you see and hear.
Notice small things.
Be moved by gentleness.
Look around yourself and inside yourself
　　and you have seen everything.

Fifty-Three

Anyone with a brain can figure out
that it is easier to drive on the highway
than through the fields and ditches.
Yet, look how many people drive off the road
when it comes to following the Way of Life.

Take a look at how rich the corporations are
and how poor the poor people.
While children live in falling-down houses,
the corporations build temples of power
and buy up more and more of the land,
consuming 'til they are swollen huge,
owning more than they can use—
these folks have driven off the road.
If you know one thing, know that this is true.

Fifty-Four

The deeper you carve your name in wood,
   the harder it is to sand away.
So, behave with integrity,
   and you are a person of integrity.
Teach integrity to your children,
   and it will last for generations.
Show integrity to your community,
   and integrity will spread.
Present it to your country,
   and your country moves ahead.
Carve it deep enough,
   and it cannot be sanded smooth.
Tell the world about the Way of Life
   and the Way shall be the rule.
How do I know it will work out this way?
Because I have seen the truth.

Fifty-Five

A woman who fills herself with the Way of Life
is reborn each moment.
Though her body is mortal,
her enemies cannot harm her,
because her grip on truth is strong.
Though she is away from her lover,
she is not half a person.
She can talk all day without tiring,
because everything she says
is in harmony with the Way of Life.

This harmony is balance,
and balance is wholeness.
To want more than wholeness
does not make sense
and it is not the Way of Life.
To go against the Way of Life
is to refuse to be reborn into this moment.

Fifty-Six

If a man talks about how much he knows
  about the Way of Life,
    he does not know the Way of Life.
Instead of talking so much,
  he should keep his mouth shut,
    examine what he believes
    and watch his temper.
He should be humble
  and live a simple and natural life.
This is to be one with the Way.
If he is one with the Way,
  his friends and enemies
    will be the same to him.
So will profit and loss,
  obscurity and fame.
If he can achieve this,
  he has reached the highest achievement.

Fifty-Seven

If you are in charge of a nation,
　be upfront.
If you are in charge of a war,
　be sneaky.
If you are in charge of the world,
　do nothing.
Why? Because:

If you enforce codes of conduct,
　they will make people misbehave.
If you build weapons,
　they will be used.
If you create a market for junk,
　people will buy it.
If you elect lawmakers,
　they will find crooks.

So tell yourself:
I'll leave people alone
　and they will mature on their own.
I won't boss them around
　and solutions will be found.
I'll keep my hands off their money
　and they'll find ways to thrive.
I'll be pleased with their behavior,
　and they'll be naturally kind.

Fifty-Eight

When the leader does not pay attention,
the people grow careless.
When the leader is overly controlling,
the people sneak around.
If you appreciate good fortune,
you must have tasted bad.
If you curse your luck,
you must have seen better days.

Opposite truths go 'round and 'round,
and as far as anyone can tell
they never end.
As soon as you think you know the truth,
the truth alludes you once again.

Be both yes and no.

Act without hesitation,
but do not interrupt.

Be the center of attention
without showing off.

Become as sharp as the blade of a knife,
but harm no one.

Fifty-Nine

A true leader is a servant
to the sons and daughters of the Way of Life.
All things are these sons and daughters.
So to be a true leader, be careful with the world.
Consider your actions, live without wasting.
To do this is to invest in your own virtue.

We know how investment works:
The longer you invest,
    the larger your investment grows.
The larger your investment,
    the more financially secure you will be.
When you are financially secure,
    you can own all the things you want.

You can't buy things
    with your virtue,
        but through your virtue
            you can know the mother of things.
Know the mother of things
    and your leadership will be
        as deeply rooted as a tree,
            as long lasting as eternity.

Sixty

A good fisherman knows
that if you handle a fish too much,
you spoil it.

A good leader knows
that to handle people too much
is to turn them against him.

Leave people alone as much as possible
and they will forget about bad history.
Or perhaps they will remember,
but in remembering,
they will not hold a grudge.
When people do not hold a grudge,
their leaders do not have to confront them.
When leaders do no confront the people,
there is peace.
When there is peace,
the leaders and the people
give credit to each other,
and they come together as one.

Sixty-One

Because a valley is a low place,
   all it has to do is be still
     and all rivers will flow into it
      like a man flows into a woman.

A large nation is like a valley.
If it puts itself in the low position,
   the services of small nations
     will flow into it,
      and the small will be part of the large.
If the small nations allow
   their services to flow into the large
     by taking the high position
      the large will become part of the small.

It makes sense then, for the larger
   nation to take the low position.

Sixty-Two

Have you ever noticed how easy it is
to say polite words without meaning them?
Or how easy it is to follow rules of politeness
without goodness in your heart?
Understanding this,
we should not think poorly of someone
who behaves with rough manners,
because politeness and manners
are meaningless.

Think about it this way:
It is considered polite
to exchange extravagant gifts
on holidays and days of celebration,
yet these gifts can be given
without any real feeling.
Instead of rushing out to purchase merchandise,
we should relax and offer the Way of Life.
The Way of Life makes a place for everyone.
One person follows It
and It makes a home for him.
Another person does not follow It,
and It makes a home for him still.
What more could you give than this?

Sixty-Three

The Way of Life says,
"Do nothing and get much done."
"Enjoy the taste of no taste."
"Know that less is more."
But how can this be so?

If a man solves a big problem,
   he had to first let the problem get big.
If a country wins a war,
   that means the leaders entered into a war
      in the first place.

Make a promise too quickly,
   and you may find yourself
      having to break it.
Take problems too lightly,
   and they will grow to have weight.
Those who follow the Way
   deal with issues before they are issues.
When it appears that they've done nothing,
   it means the work started out complete.

Sixty-Four

Pay attention,
  and deal with things
    before they develop.
The enemy you never make
  is the quickest one to call a truce;
The easiest weed to pull
  is the weed that doesn't take root.

The tallest tree started as a sapling.
The highest mountain has its base
  in a pile of dirt.
The longest journey
  starts with one footstep,
    and big problems
      can be solved when they are small
        if you put in a little work.

Therefore, a wise person does little work.

However:
Projects never fail in the planning stages.
It is when they are near completion
  that things start to go wrong.
So pay as much attention
  to the ending as the beginning
    when you are trying to get things done.

Followers of the Way of Life
  desire to not desire.
They want to not want expensive things.
They know by knowing they know nothing,
  and they find value in what others
    leave behind.

Sixty-Five

A long time ago,
   when all rulers ruled by the Way of Life,
     they did not use their authority
      to tell people how to think.
Instead, they let people live free
   of this kind of teaching.
When people are free
   from the teachings of leaders,
     they are peaceful
      and they govern themselves.
Leaders who rule by the book
   are poor leaders.
Leaders who rule with natural understandings
   are good.
Use this as a model for leadership
   and you will find a mysterious truth:
If you "understand" rather than "know,"
   you are not one of many
     but one with the whole.

Sixty-Six

Some people say that
   the sea is the lord of the river.
This is because the river
   seeks the lower level of the sea.
If you wish to lead, therefore,
   you should place yourself lower than people
      and they will seek your guidance
         naturally.
Don't bully your way to the front of the line,
   stand last in line, instead.
When speaking to people, be honest and simple,
   instead of making a lot of double-talk
      fly above their heads.

Do this and people will not fear your authority.
They will not complain about your bossy ways.
Instead, they will gladly follow your directions,
   and believe the things you have to say.

Followers of the Way of Life
   never lose an argument
      because they do not argue with people.

Sixty-Seven

Lots of people say
the Way of Life makes no sense,
but if the Way of Life
made sense to people
it would have long ago
become small and ordinary.

But the Way of Life is not small and ordinary.
It is full of treasures
like compassion,
moderation,
and service to others.

When I am moved to feel compassion,
I have the courage to do the right thing.
When I live with moderation,
I find that I have more.
When I put the needs of others before mine,
I am made a leader.
The Way offers these three treasures
like gemstones washed ashore.

But if I demonstrate courage without compassion,
or if I use up resources and won't slow my pace,
or if I make myself a leader without first
serving others,
I'm asking for death—because this is
not the Way.

Treasure compassion.
It has heaven inside it.

Sixty-Eight

The most successful warriors don't go to war.
The best fighters are those
  who turn down invitations to fight.
The greatest champions among us
  don't seek competition.
The best employers serve their workers
  and respect them—
    they don't manage them with might.
There is power in stepping back from power—
  in dealing with people, this is best.
It is the natural way, the way of heaven,
  and joining with heaven brings success.

Sixty-Nine

The ancient warriors had a saying:
It is better to take an attack than to make one.
It is better to back up than to advance.
Take action by taking no action.
Be strong by using no strength.
Take to arms without picking up weapons.
Attacking a peaceful person
    will be your enemy's greatest mistake.

When someone attacks a peaceful person,
    no matter what is gained,
        what he loses is compassion,
            and when compassion is lost,
                nothing of importance remains.

Compassion contains heaven.
He who loses everything but heaven wins all.

Seventy

What I say is easy to believe,
  but few believe it.
Without hearing my words,
  or witnessing my deeds,
    they wave their hands and dismiss me.
Others pretend to understand,
  but this only makes a mockery of my wisdom.
Those who understand don't put on airs
  with fancy clothes and jewelry.
They wear their gemstones on the inside.

Seventy-One

What is better—
to know much while believing you know little,
or to know little while believing
you know much?

I'll tell you.
If you believe you know much
when you know little,
that is a sickness.
It will prevent you from learning,
because at every opportunity to learn,
you will say, "I already know
what I need to know."
You must become aware of this sickness,
and be sickened by it,
for it to be cured.

Know more by understanding
how little you know.

Seventy-Two

There are awesome things
    that should be respected—
        like the sea.
To not respect the sea can lead to disaster.
But a good leader does not command
    this kind of fear.
He does not confine people
    to their homes,
        or force them into hard labor.
He trusts them to come and go
    and work as they see fit.
People do not get tired of a leader like this.
Therefore, those who follow
    the Way of Life
        know their power but do not show it.
They think well of themselves
    but do not place themselves
        in positions of honor.
In adopting this way
    they leave fear where it should be—
        in the awesome powers of the sea.

Seventy-Three

Daring can lead to death.
Safe living keeps you alive.
Both these ways can be right,
   both can be wrong.
Who knows why the Way of Life
   holds these double truths?
Even the smartest people in the world
   don't understand how heaven works.
Heaven goes forward without moving.
It doesn't have a voice,
   but answers our questions.
It never stops working, yet is relaxed.
It doesn't call for us, yet we come.
Heaven casts a net
   that not one thing slips through.

Seventy-Four

Because people naturally fear death,
    threats of death can be used to control them.
If people are put to death
    for different ways of thinking,
    who will dare to think differently?

All people will reach death naturally,
    so nature is the master of death.
If I try to cut wood like a master carpenter,
    I just end up cutting my hand.
If I try to take nature into my own hands and
    bring death to others,
    I harm myself.
The work of a master
    should be left to the master.

Seventy-Five

A small percentage of people
  control a large percentage of wealth and power.
Because of this,
  most people live in powerless poverty.
When people live in powerless poverty,
  they have nothing to lose.
When people have nothing to lose,
  they are fearless of rebelling.
When they are fearless of rebelling,
  death holds no power over them.
When death holds no power over people,
  they are able to live more fully
    than those who spend their lives
      so content with wealth and power
        that they are afraid to die.

Seventy-Six

People are soft when they are born;
  they stiffen when they die.
Plants are tender when they sprout;
  in death they become brittle and dry.

To live according to unbending rules
  is to behave like things that have died.
To allow your rules to be flexible
  is to let them be alive.

It is the brittle tree that is cut for wood.
The army that never yields is doomed.
Rigid things will fall away
  to be replaced by the soft and new.

Seventy-Seven

An archer's bow stretches
  where it needs to stretch,
    becoming long where it was short.
The Way of Life stretches like this, too,
  letting the high become the low.
It takes from what is plentiful
  to make up for what is scarce.
The way of money is a different way,
  because wealth attracts more wealth.

Is there anyone who has so much,
  that when she gives all she has away,
    she finds that she has even more?
Yes, that is a person of the Way.

She does good work to do good work,
  not because of how much she's paid.
She shares because she wants to share,
  not because she's seeking praise.
She lets the high become the low
  and weakness become her strength.

Seventy-Eight

There is nothing more willing
　to change than water.
It becomes the shape of its container
　without resisting.
Yet water can overwhelm
　the strongest swimmer
　　and erase stone from existence.

It is the weakness of water
　that takes over the strong.
And though everyone knows it is true—
　that the softness of water
　　is what conquers the hard—
　　　few know how to live by this rule.

To live like water, don't argue, don't resist;
　take the shape you need to take.
Accept responsibility for each situation
　no matter where there's fault or blame.

Understand—
　truth often sounds like the opposite of truth.

Seventy-Nine

After long drawn-out disputes,
  no settlement satisfies everyone,
  and resentment is sure to linger.
So how can there ever be peace?
People who follow the Way know—
  peace comes to those who are easy to please.
They accept the resolution offered
  and don't quibble over tiny details,
    while people who do not follow the Way
    make demands and dig in their heels.

The Way of Life does not care who you are.
If you are easy to please,
  it leads you toward peace.

Eighty

In simple times,
   people know each other well.
Though they travel, they return.
Though they have locks on their doors,
   they don't use them.

In simple times,
   all people are needed to do the work,
     and in doing valuable work,
       all people find their jobs satisfying.

In simple times,
   people are satisfied with simple things—
     simple food, simple dress—
     and in being so satisfied,
       they feel no need to meddle
       in the affairs of those
       living nearby.

Eighty-One

The truth is not always pretty,
    what is pretty is not always true.
Mature people do not need to argue;
    those who argue are rarely mature.

People who follow the Way of Life
    don't flaunt their credentials.
They don't need to accumulate wealth.
They give away what they have to others,
    and in doing so, add to themselves.

The Way of Life gives Itself away
    but never becomes less than everything.
Those who follow It accomplish everything
    by giving themselves away.

Sources

I read many translation of the *Tao Te Ching* while I was working on this book. I cannot say that any particular text was a source for any particular verse, only that each one of the following books informed the work in general.

Bynner, Witter. *The Way of Life According to Lao Tzu.* New York: Capricorn Books, 1944.

Cleary, Thomas. *The Essential Tao.* San Francisco: HarperSanFrancisco, 1993.

Lao Tzu. *Tao Te Ching.* Gia-Fu Feng and Jane English, trans. New York: Vintage Books, 1972.

———. *Tao Te Ching.* D. C. Lau, trans. Baltimore: Penguin Classics, 1963.

Le Guin, Ursula K. *Lao Tzu: Tao Te Ching: A Book about the Way and the Power of the Way.* Boston: Shambhala, 1997.

Shoenewolf, Gerald. *The Way: According to Lao Tzu, Chaung Tzu and Seng Tsan.* Fremont, CA: Jain, 2000.

About the Author

Susan Montag has been a teacher, writer, and editor. She grew up in southern Iowa where she developed the Midwestern sensibility often found in her fiction. Montag was the editor of the literary magazine *Midday Moon* and is the author of a collection of short fiction, *Nude Ascending a Staircase*, published by Bellowing Ark Press in 2001. She lives in Minnesota with her husband Roger and her two children, Matthew and Emma. She has a Master of Fine Arts from Hamline University, St. Paul.